P9-CCM-740

I didn't know that

sharks

keep

losing

their

teeth

© Aladdin Books Ltd 1998
© U.S. text 1998
Produced by
Aladdin Books Ltd
28 Percy Street
London W1P 0LD

First published in the United States in 1998 by
Copper Beech Books,
an imprint of
The Millbrook Press
2 Old New Milford Road
Brookfield, Connecticut 06804

Concept, editorial, and design by
David West Children's Books
Designer: Robert Perry
Illustrators: Darren Harvey – Wildlife Art Ltd.,
Jo Moore

10 9 8 7 6 (trade : hc.)
10 9 8 7 6 5 4 3 2 (lib. bdg.)

Library of Congress Cataloging-in-Publication Data
Llewellyn, Claire.
Sharks keep losing their teeth and other amazing facts about sharks / by Claire
Llewellyn ; illustrated by Darren Harvey and Jo Moore.
p. cm. — (I didn't know that—)
Includes index.
Summary: Provides information about the diet, anatomy, habits, and
reproduction of sharks.
ISBN 0-7613-0646-3 (trade : hc.). — ISBN 0-7613-0712-5 (lib. bdg.)
1. Sharks—Juvenile literature. [1. Sharks.] I. Harvey, Darren, ill.
II. Moore, Jo, ill. III. Title. IV. Series.
QL638.9.L58 1998   97-41606
597.3—dc21   CIP AC

I didn't know that

sharks keep losing their teeth

Claire Llewellyn

COPPER BEECH BOOKS
BROOKFIELD, CONNECTICUT

I didn't know that

Introduction

Did *you* know that some sharks are older than dinosaurs? ... that most sharks are smaller than you? ... that some grow inside mermaids' purses?

Discover for yourself amazing facts about sharks – what they eat, how they have babies, who their enemies are, and more.

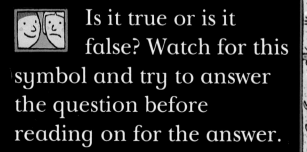

 Watch for this symbol that means there is a fun project for you to try.

Is it true or is it false? Watch for this symbol and try to answer the question before reading on for the answer.

I didn't know that

sharks are older than dinosaurs. Sharks' ancestors lived about 200 million years before the dinosaurs. Some were giants and had spines on their heads.

Can you find five trilobites?

Few sharks turned into *fossils*, but their teeth did! This tooth (left) measures 12 inches and belonged to a monster shark called megalodon. A great white shark's tooth is half this size.

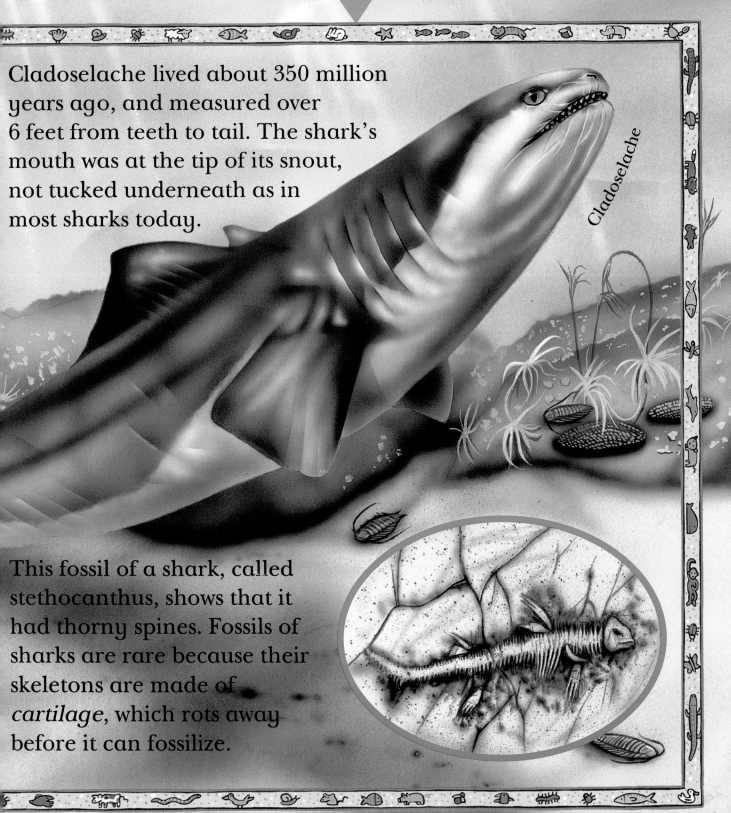

Cladoselache lived about 350 million years ago, and measured over 6 feet from teeth to tail. The shark's mouth was at the tip of its snout, not tucked underneath as in most sharks today.

Cladoselache

This fossil of a shark, called stethocanthus, shows that it had thorny spines. Fossils of sharks are rare because their skeletons are made of *cartilage*, which rots away before it can fossilize.

 To see how big a whale shark really is, try making one in the park or on the beach. Using a yardstick as a guide, measure out its length, and then fill in the outline with pebbles or twigs.

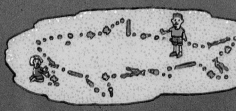

The basking shark is the world's second largest fish. It swims with its mouth open, to catch microscopic sea creatures.

8

I didn't know that

sharks are the biggest fish.

The whale shark measures up to 42 feet, and is the largest fish in the sea. This gentle giant feeds peacefully, filtering tiny plants and animals from the water.

SEARCH & FIND
Can you find three divers?
FIND & SEARCH

Whale shark

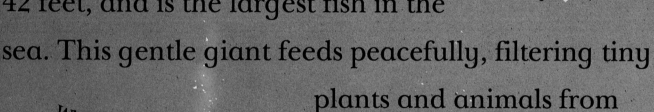

The dwarf shark is just 6 inches long, not much bigger than a goldfish. In fact, half of all known sharks measure less than three feet.

Whale sharks are so gentle that divers can ride on them.

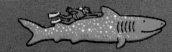

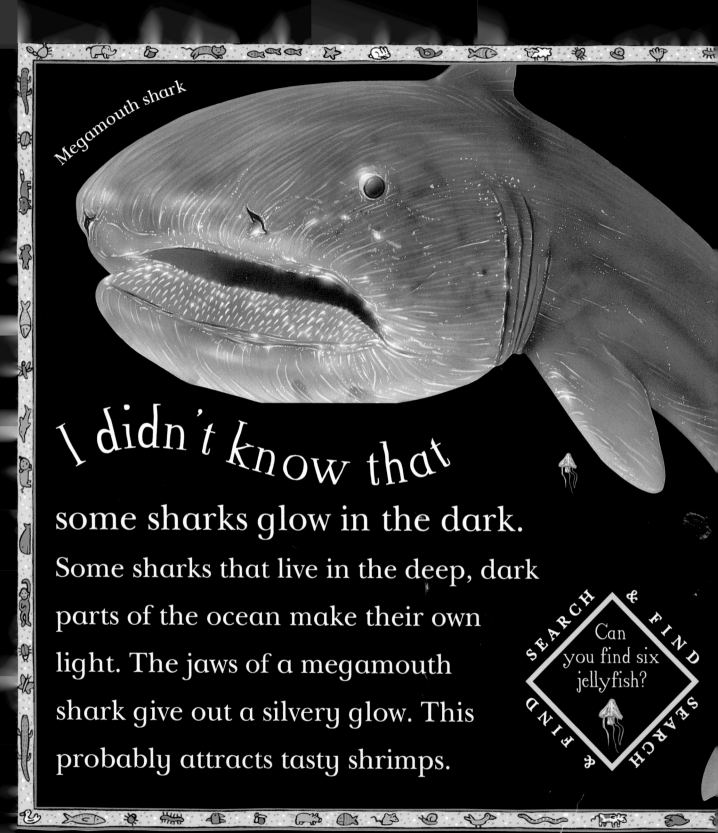

Megamouth shark

I didn't know that

some sharks glow in the dark. Some sharks that live in the deep, dark parts of the ocean make their own light. The jaws of a megamouth shark give out a silvery glow. This probably attracts tasty shrimps.

SEARCH & FIND

Can you find six jellyfish?

FIND & SEARCH

The frilled shark has elongated eyes to see in the murky depths.

The goblin shark (above right) lives at the bottom of the sea. Its long, sensitive snout helps it to find any prey nearby.

Sensitive snout

Lantern sharks (left) glow in the water thanks to a luminous slime on their skin. Experts think the coloring may help sharks to attract their prey or keep their place in a *shoal.*

The cookie-cutter shark gets its name from its curious bite. When the shark attacks another animal, it leaves a wound that is perfectly round – just like a cookie.

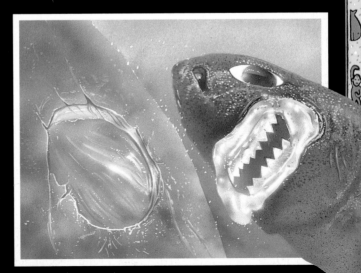

The wobbegong is a strange-looking shark with speckled skin and tassels that make it look like a rock or seaweed. The fish makes use of this *camouflage* by hiding on the ocean floor and snapping up fish.

Stingray

Gill slits

Sharks are related to *rays* (right). Both groups of fish have gill slits instead of flaps, and skeletons of cartilage rather than bone.

True or false?
Some sharks have wings.

Answer: **True**
The angel shark's large fins (left) are just like wings. It uses them to glide along the ocean floor as it searches for *crustaceans* and fish.

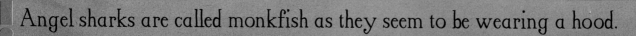
Angel sharks are called monkfish as they seem to be wearing a hood.

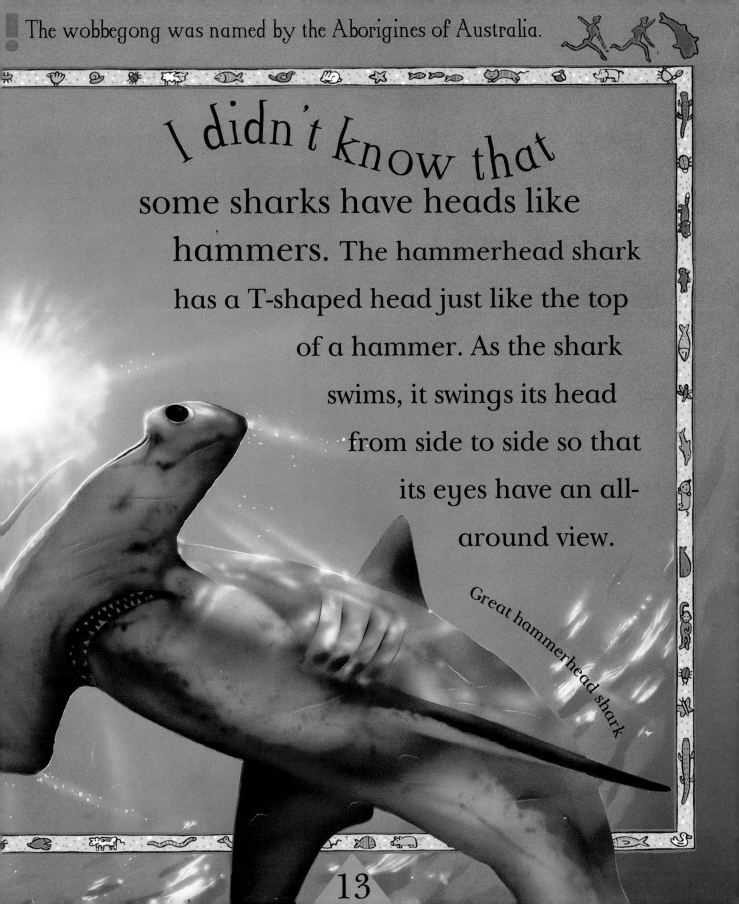

I didn't know that some sharks have heads like hammers. The hammerhead shark has a T-shaped head just like the top of a hammer. As the shark swims, it swings its head from side to side so that its eyes have an all-around view.

Great hammerhead shark

Tail fin

Dorsal fin

Pelvic fin

Pectoral fin

A shark's body is sleek, *streamlined,* and built for speed. Its fins are large and rather stiff, and help it to move forward, stay upright, steer, and stop.

Like all fish, sharks have gills to take in oxygen from water. As water flows over the gills, tiny blood vessels absorb the oxygen and carry it around the body.

Mako shark

I didn't know that

if sharks stop swimming, they sink. Most fish have an air-filled bag called a swim bladder inside them, which helps to keep them afloat in the sea. Sharks don't have swim bladders. To avoid sinking, most sharks have to swim all the time – just like treading water.

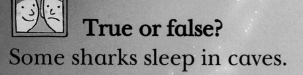

True or false?
Some sharks sleep in caves.

Answer: **True**
The whitetip reef shark is a sleepy fish. At night, it cruises sluggishly around coral reefs, and spends the day sleeping on the ocean floor. It often hides away in caves to avoid being spotted and disturbed.

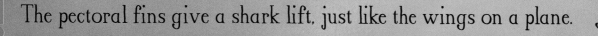

The pectoral fins give a shark lift, just like the wings on a plane.

I didn't know that

sharks keep losing their teeth. Sharks often lose their teeth as they attack their prey, so new teeth constantly grow inside their mouths. Slowly the new teeth form and move outward to replace the older ones.

SEARCH & FIND & SEARCH & FIND

Can you find five teeth?

Sand tiger shark

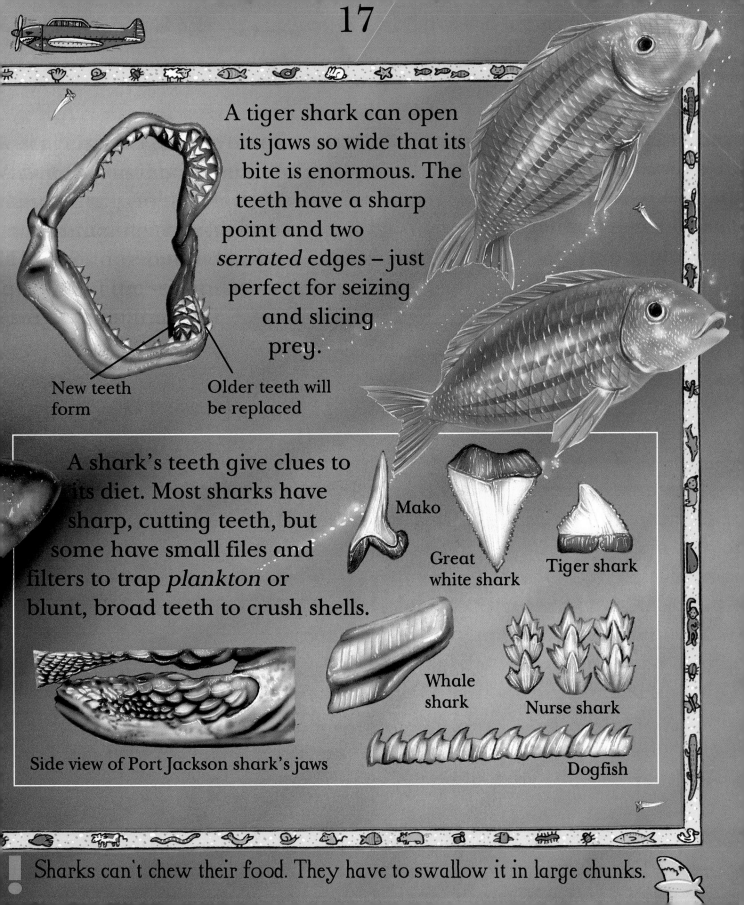

A tiger shark can open its jaws so wide that its bite is enormous. The teeth have a sharp point and two *serrated* edges – just perfect for seizing and slicing prey.

New teeth form

Older teeth will be replaced

A shark's teeth give clues to its diet. Most sharks have sharp, cutting teeth, but some have small files and filters to trap *plankton* or blunt, broad teeth to crush shells.

Mako

Great white shark

Tiger shark

Whale shark

Nurse shark

Side view of Port Jackson shark's jaws

Dogfish

Sharks can't chew their food. They have to swallow it in large chunks.

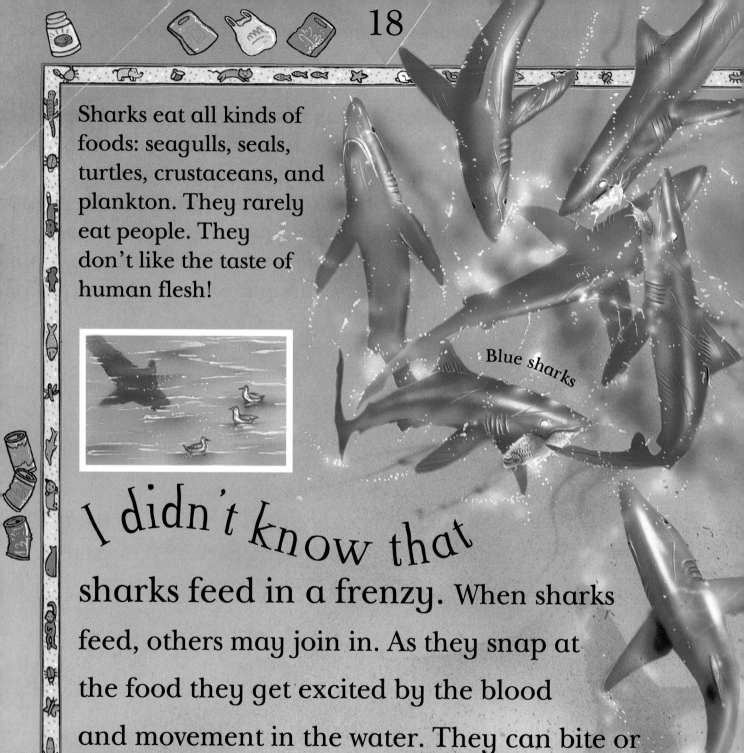

Sharks eat all kinds of foods: seagulls, seals, turtles, crustaceans, and plankton. They rarely eat people. They don't like the taste of human flesh!

Blue sharks

I didn't know that sharks feed in a frenzy. When sharks feed, others may join in. As they snap at the food they get excited by the blood and movement in the water. They can bite or kill each other during this "feeding frenzy."

Found in the stomachs of sharks: a mustard jar, plastic bag, beer cans...

A shark's jaws lie a long way under its pointed snout. As the fish lunges to bite, it lifts its nose out of the way, and swings its jaws forward. Then it rolls up its eyes inside its head to protect them during the attack.

True or false?
Some sharks attack with their tail.

Answer: **True**
The thresher shark has a long tail, which it lashes in the water like a whip. Scientists think that this either stuns its prey or herds fish into a tightly-knit group, which the thresher shark then attacks.

Sharks have a good sense of taste and spit out things that are bad.

Sharks have a lateral line on each side of their body, which picks up *vibrations* in the sea. It helps sharks to feel the things that are moving around them, such as a seal or a fish.

Oceanic whitetip shark

SEARCH & FIND
Can you find the other fish?
FIND & SEARCH

A shark's body is covered, not with scales, but with toothlike bumps called denticles. These are very coarse, and feel rough if they're stroked the wrong way.

I didn't know that

sharks can smell blood over a half mile away. Sharks have a keen sense of smell. As water streams past their nostrils, they pick up messages in the sea around them. Some sharks can sniff the blood of a wounded animal over a half mile away, and race toward it.

Sharks have tiny *organs* on their snout that can pick up electrical signals. Since every creature in the sea produces some kind of electricity, these organs help sharks to hunt them down.

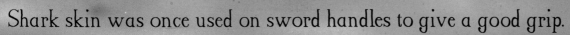

Shark skin was once used on sword handles to give a good grip.

I didn't know that

some fish hitch rides on sharks.
Remoras are small fish with a sucker
pad on their heads. They use it to cling
on to sharks. As they ride, they help by
eating *parasites* on the sharks' skin.

Sucker
pad

Like surfers, remoras ride on the waves made by sharks.

Long *tapeworms* live inside a shark's stomach and steal its food.

Small, agile pilot fish often swim alongside a shark. They probably feel safe near their large companion, and can also feed on scraps of its food.

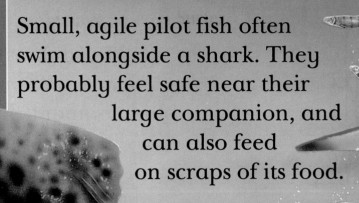

Zebra shark

SEARCH & FIND
Can you find ten remoras?
FIND SEARCH &

Copepods are crustaceans that stick to a shark's fins and feed on it. They may even cling to a shark's eyes, so that it can hardly see.

Sharks' eggs hatch more quickly in warm water.

I didn't know that

some baby sharks grow inside mermaids' purses. Some sharks lay their eggs in leathery cases called mermaids' purses. Inside the purses, the eggs grow into baby sharks. They eat the *yolk* and hatch ten months later.

SEARCH & FIND & SEARCH & FIND

Can you find the mother shark?

Swell shark embryos
Three months old
Seven months old

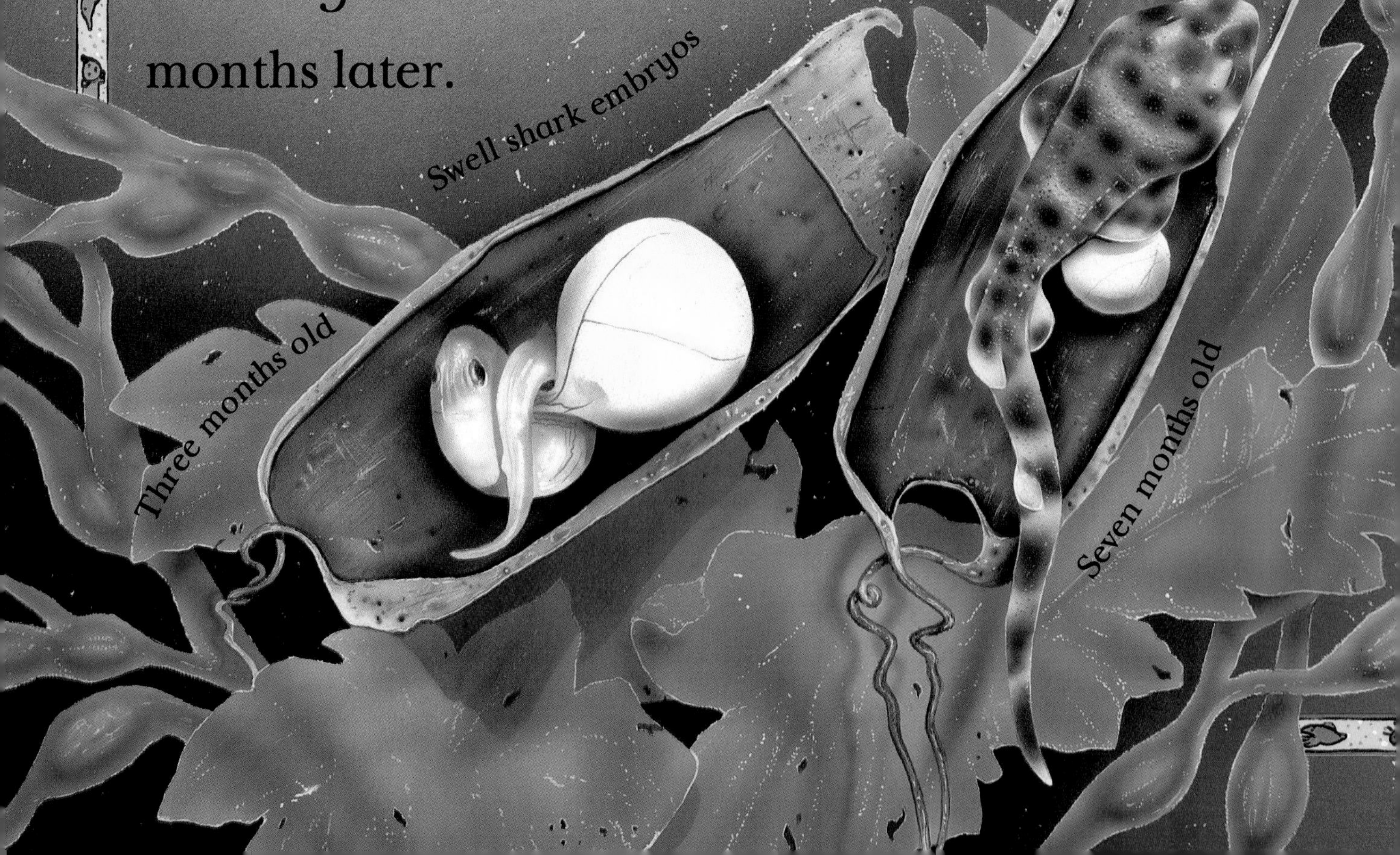

While some sharks hatch out of eggs, most develop inside their mother's body. They feed either on egg yolk or on food in their mother's blood, and are later born live, like *mammals*.

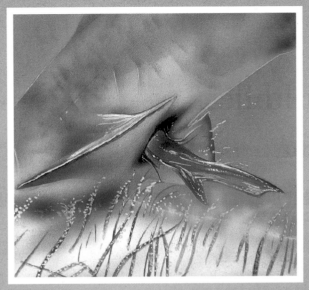

A baby lemon shark emerges from its mother.

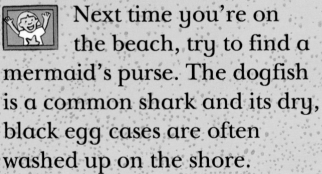

Next time you're on the beach, try to find a mermaid's purse. The dogfish is a common shark and its dry, black egg cases are often washed up on the shore.

Many sharks try to protect their eggs. The horn shark wedges her spiral-shaped egg case into a crack in a rock. Other egg cases have long tendrils that cling to plants.

Horn shark egg

A whale shark's egg is the size of a football.

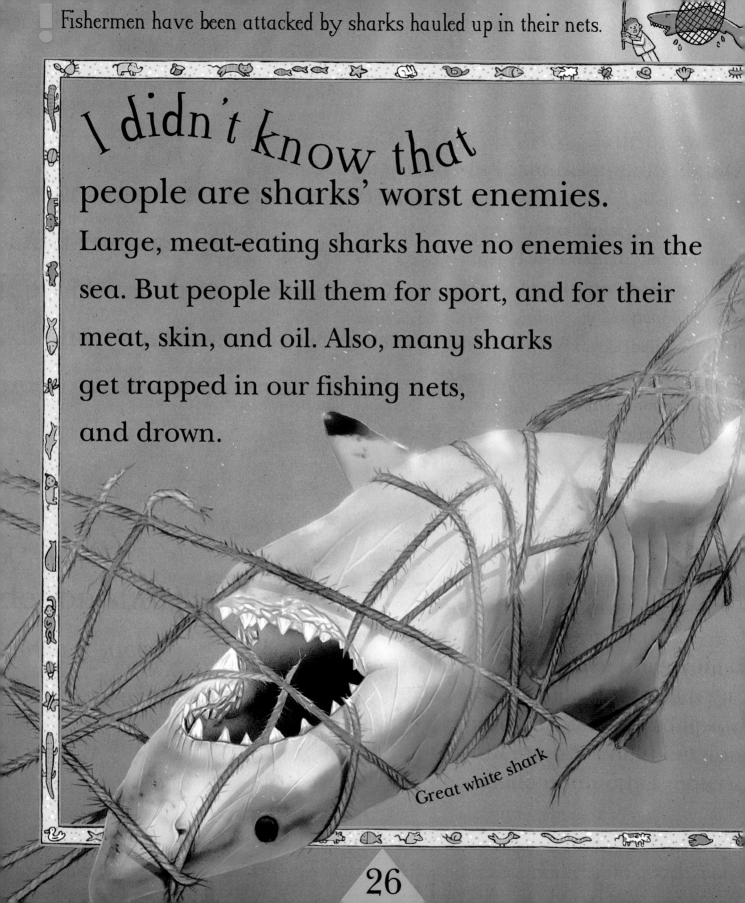

I didn't know that

people are sharks' worst enemies. Large, meat-eating sharks have no enemies in the sea. But people kill them for sport, and for their meat, skin, and oil. Also, many sharks get trapped in our fishing nets, and drown.

Great white shark

True or false?

Sharks are blood-thirsty killers.

Answer: **False**

This is a myth that movies, such as *Jaws*, have helped to spread. Most sharks leave people alone. Scientists believe that attacks only happen when a shark mistakes a swimmer for a seal or other kind of prey.

Surfer

Seal

Bull shark

Sharks die so that people can make soup from their fins, jewelry from their teeth, and medicines and lipsticks from their oil. Yet all these things can be made using other materials.

Some people catch sharks for sport, and treat their bodies as trophies. Every year, the number of large sharks in the sea falls.

Shark liver oil pills

Jewelry

Shark fin soup

Cosmetics

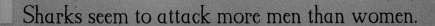

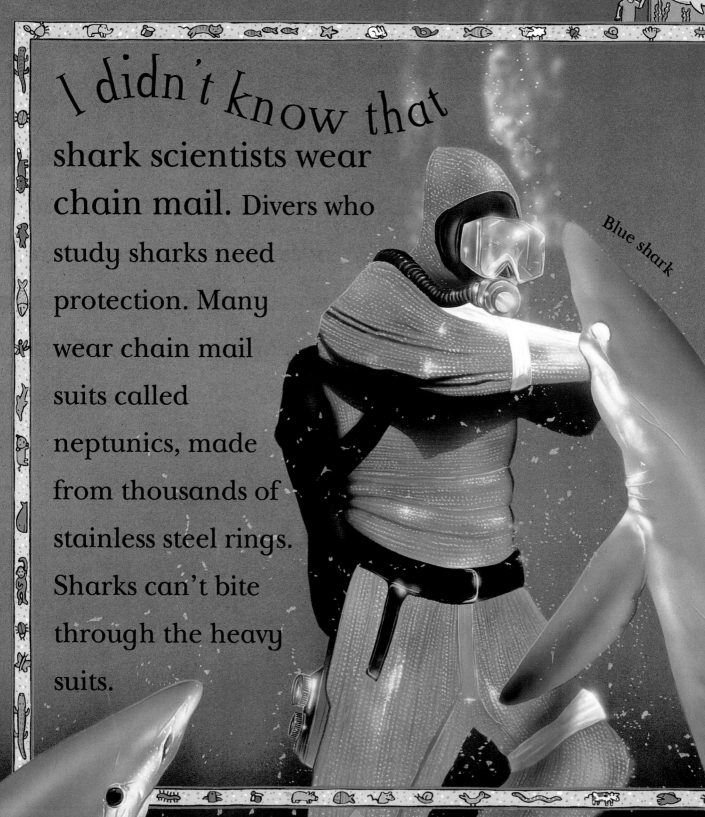

I didn't know that

shark scientists wear chain mail. Divers who study sharks need protection. Many wear chain mail suits called neptunics, made from thousands of stainless steel rings. Sharks can't bite through the heavy suits.

Blue shark

Sonic tag

Tiger shark

To study sharks, scientists need to be able to follow them. They do this by catching sharks, attaching sonic tags to their fins and then returning them to the water. The tags give out radio signals that the scientists carefully track.

Tagging pole

Underwater photographers can film sharks safely from inside strong metal cages. It can still be a scary ordeal, though. They attract the sharks with a strong-smelling *bait*. Sometimes the sharks crash heavily against the cages, trying to get inside!

Great white shark

The bubbles from a diver's Aqua-Lung scare some sharks.

Glossary

Bait
Food, such as a dead fish, which is used to attract sharks.

Camouflage
The colors and markings on an animal that help it to blend in with its surroundings.

Cartilage
The material that forms the skeletons of sharks and rays.

Crustacean
An animal, such as a lobster or a crab, that has a hard outer shell and lots of legs.

Fossil
Animal remains that have turned to stone over millions of years.

Hibernate
To spend the winter in a kind of deep sleep.

Mammal
An animal, such as a cat, that gives birth to its young and nourishes it with milk.

Organ
Any part of the body that has a special purpose, such as the eyes that are the organs of sight and the ears that are the organs of hearing.

Parasites
Animals that live on other animals (known as hosts) and gets food from them. A parasite always damages its host.

Plankton
Microscopic plants and animals that live in the sea.

Ray
A large, flat sea fish with winglike fins and a long tail.

Serrated
Having a sharp, zig-zagging edge like a saw.

Shoal
A large group or school of fish.

Streamlined
Having a smooth body shape that moves easily through the water.

Tapeworm
A long, flat worm that lives inside the stomach and intestines of other animals. It is a parasite.

Yolk
The yellow part inside an egg that provides food for the growing animal.

Index

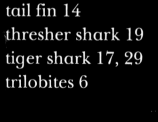

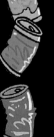